ICE MAN

About the author

Michael Smith gave up his career as a leading business and political journalist to write the bestselling biography, *An Unsung Hero – Tom Crean, Antarctic Explorer*. He has a life-long interest in Polar exploration and has also written *I Am Just Going Outside – Captain Oates, Antarctic Tragedy*. This is his first book for children.

About the Illustrator

Annie Brady is a student at The National College of Art and Design, Dublin and works as a freelance illustrator. These are her first published illustrations.

ICE MAN

The Remarkable Adventures of Antarctic Explorer Tom Crean

Michael Smith

Illustrations by Annie Brady

The Collins Press

First published 2003 by
The Collins Press,
West Link Park,
Doughcloyne,
Wilton,
Cork

© Text Michael Smith
© Original drawings Annie Brady

Michael Smith has asserted his right to be identified as author of this book
British Library Cataloguing in Publication data.

ISBN: 1-903464-44-7

Printed in Ireland by ColourBooks Ltd.
Design by Artmark

CONTENTS

INTRODUCTION

Far away at the very bottom of the world in the harsh ice-covered continent of Antarctica stands a dark mountain. It towers above the endless plains of snow and ice.

The mountain is called Mount Crean[1] and it stands as a lasting monument to a remarkable man whose name will forever be linked with the first exploration to the unknown Antarctic continent. His name was Tom Crean.

Tom Crean was among the small band of outstanding men who conquered the unexplored Antarctic wilderness about 100 years ago. His astonishing adventures helped lift the veil from Antarctica and no history of the frozen land can be written without saluting the massive role he played.

Tom Crean sailed on three great expeditions to the region when it was largely unknown and he spent longer on the ice than more famous explorers like Captain Robert Scott or Sir Ernest Shackleton.

But his incredible exploits were half-forgotten and overlooked for almost 100 years. He was the unknown hero of Antarctic exploration.

This is a stirring tale of an ordinary man who rose from humble beginnings on an Irish farm to become a legendary figure of Antarctic exploration.

People are eager for heroes and Tom Crean is a hero for every age.

[1.] Tom Crean's name will live forever in the Antarctic, where two landmarks have been named after him. Mount Crean is located in Victoria Land, map reference: 77.90°S – 159.47° W and stands 2.5km (1.5 miles or 8,360ft high). The Crean Glacier is on the island of South Georgia, map reference: 54.17°S – 28.13°W.

Note: In Tom Crean's time, a different system of measuring distance and weights was used. In this book modern measures are used with the older conversions shown in brackets. Temperatures are given in Celsius with the Fahrenheit comparison shown in brackets. See page 124 for useful comparisons.

Chapter 1

A FARMER'S LAD

Half a world away from the frozen Antarctic's ice and snow are the lush, green fields of Ireland. The contrast between the two different landscapes is stark – one is always cold, hostile and alien to humans, while the other is mild, grassy and welcoming.

However, it was a man from Ireland's soft rolling hills who tamed the world's most wild and violent place, Antarctica. The man was Tom Crean.

Tom's story began over 100 years ago. He was born in 1877 near the village of Anascaul in County Kerry on Ireland's western shores.

Tom had a humble start in life. His parents were very poor farmers who struggled to work the land and feed their ten children.

Life on the farm was extremely hard. There were no luxuries like electricity or telephones, people were often hungry and when crops failed many thousands died. Only the toughest survived.

Children like Tom had little chance to escape the poverty. Schools were poor and children learned little more than how to read and write. They often left school by the age of twelve, too early to develop skills or knowledge and find a good job.

But Tom was a determined lad. He wanted more than a life of struggle and dreamt of better times. The chance came in the summer of 1893, when he was just fifteen years old.

One day, Tom's father asked him to work in a potato field. Potatoes were the basic diet for Irish people at the time and looking after the crop was a matter of life and death for farmers and their families.

But Tom was daydreaming. Without thinking, he left the gate to the field wide open and, in a moment, some cows wandered into the field and started eating the precious potatoes.

Tom's father was furious and shouted at his dozy son. Father and son had a blazing row and an angry Tom swore that he would run away from home.

A few days later Tom was strolling along by the seashore near his home when he came across a man in a uniform chatting to some local people. The man was a recruiting officer for the British navy and Tom listened to what the officer had to say.

Britain's navy in Victorian times was the most powerful in the world and it needed an endless supply of young men to crew the vast fleet of ships which cruised the oceans.

Ireland was one of the places where recruiting officers came to find new sailors and for many young Irish lads, a job in the navy was their best chance of getting away from the struggle on the land.

The Atlantic coastline of Kerry is the most westerly point in Europe and the local people have long connections with the sea. Going to sea was a normal step.

Tom was brought up in Kerry with tales of seafaring exploits, including those of the legendary St Brendan the Navigator who in the sixth century sailed into the Atlantic from Brandon Creek – only a few miles from where Tom grew up many centuries later.

Tom's lucky meeting with the naval recruiting officer was his chance to follow in the footsteps of St Brendan and the Kerry tradition.

He strode up to the officer and asked how he could enlist in the navy. To his dismay the officer said recruits had to be sixteen years of age.

Tom was only fifteen but he was determined to run away. So he lied. In an instant, he told the British officer he was sixteen. No more questions were asked and Tom was promptly enrolled as a junior seaman in Queen Victoria's mighty Royal Navy.

Tom raced back home to break the news to his parents. In some circumstances, his parents might have stopped him going, especially since he was so young. But it was one mouth less left to feed on the farm and Tom's parents allowed him to go.

Tom had other problems. First his clothes were scruffy rags he wore to work on the farm. Second, he did not have any money saved to pay his train fare to the naval port at Cobh, near Cork city.

Luckily a kind soul lent him a small sum for the train ticket and he borrowed a shirt, jacket and trousers from someone else. The fresh-faced fifteen-year-old stepped down the hill to a new life at sea, never to return to his life on the farm.

It was the first time the young Kerryman stepped into the unknown. But it was not the last.

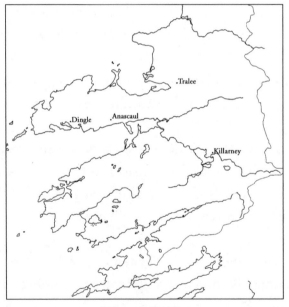

Anascaul, Co. Kerry

Chapter 2

A STEP INTO THE UNKNOWN

Tom Crean was a scrawny teenager when he joined the navy and he found that life was hard for ordinary sailors. He started his new career at the lowest rank, known as Boy 2nd Class and was sent to a training ship to learn the ropes.

Work was demanding, the discipline was very strict and 700 or 800 men were crammed together below decks on big naval battleships. Although the food was not good, it was probably better than Tom had at home.

Below decks a heavy cloud of tobacco smoke hung over the men's living quarters, since most sailors puffed a pipe all day long. At night hundreds of sailors slept in hammocks strung out like rows of clothes' lines.

But eight years later in 1901, Tom's life in the navy changed forever.

Tom's battleship, the *HMS Ringarooma*, was on duty patrolling in the Pacific Ocean. By chance the vessel happened to be moored in New Zealand just before Christmas. Over the horizon came another vessel, the British exploration ship, *Discovery*, which moored alongside the *Ringarooma* in the harbour.

Discovery was Captain Robert Scott's special ice ship en route to

explore the unknown continent of Antarctic. Tom and his fellow sailors eagerly rushed on deck to catch a sight of the famous craft before it disappeared into unexplored waters.

Discovery was in New Zealand to pick up last-minute supplies of food and equipment before starting the long journey south. But plans were disrupted when one of Captain Scott's sailors got drunk and attacked an officer. To avoid punishment, the sailor fled.

Captain Scott urgently needed a replacement for the deserter and asked the *Ringarooma's* captain if he could spare one of his sailors. On board the *Ringarooma*, Tom heard the news and bravely offered to replace the runaway sailor.

By this stage, the skinny teenager who ran away from home in 1893 had developed into a fine, strapping seaman, standing close to 1.8m (6ft). Captain Scott was impressed by the big Irishman and was happy to welcome Tom on board *Discovery*.

Once again, Tom was stepping into the unknown – this time as an Antarctic explorer.

Chapter 3

FOOTPRINTS IN THE SNOW

Antarctica was almost unknown to the outside world as Tom Crean prepared for his long sea journey of 3,200km (2,000 miles) to uncharted land. Large gaps still existed in the maps and few people had any knowledge of what lay ahead on the journey.

Only a handful of men had set foot on the continent by 1901 and these early invaders did not stray very far from the shore. No one had explored the middle of the country and no one knew what they might find when they travelled towards the South Pole.

People knew far more about the Moon before American astronauts made the first landing in 1969 than the early explorers knew about Antarctica in 1901.

But this mysterious frozen land had a special place in people's minds. The Antarctic was unusual because it was always believed the continent existed – even before people set eyes on the land.

The mystery of Antarctica can be traced back to ancient times. Wise Greek scholars were the first to suggest that the earth was round.

The Greeks also knew that land existed at the top of the earth in the northern regions. For balance, they insisted, another chunk of land had to exist at the bottom of the globe. They were convinced a continent lay in the southern regions – even though it had never been seen.

It was this belief which led to the continent being named Antarctica. Land in the north was called *Arktos* (Greek for 'bear') because the region lies beneath the well-known bright stars in the constellation of The Bear. As a result, the great unknown land in the south was called *Antarktikos* – the opposite of *Arktos*.

Once explorers finally reached the land, they found the conditions were worse than anyone imagined. Antarctica was not meant for humans.

They discovered a bitterly cold, very windy and highly dangerous place where nothing grew. There were no plants or wildlife to provide food that would keep people alive.

The cold, extreme weather poses the biggest threat to life. During winter temperatures sink below -40° Celsius (-40° Fahrenheit) and -70°C (-94°F) is common. Even in the warmer summer months -30°C (-22°F) can be expected. Once, the thermometer plunged to -89.6° C (-129°F), the coldest level ever recorded on earth.

It is so cold that boiling water poured from a kettle would freeze before hitting the ground. By contrast, a typical freezer in today's homes is usually set at around -20°C (-4°F), or higher than temperatures taken during the warmest summer weather in Antarctica.

Blizzards and howling winds are another vicious factor in the climate.

Winds can rise to 320kph (200mph), about as fast as today's high-speed trains. On a normal day winds can screech to 80kph (50mph) and it is difficult for people to stand up straight under the blitz.

The impact of the wind, called wind-chill, can be highly dangerous and cause nasty frostbite. Each mile per hour in wind speed is equal to a fall of 1° in the temperature. Exposed skin freezes in a matter of seconds when winds surge above 40kph (25mph) in very low temperatures.

The only animal life, which could provide meat for the explorers, were seals and penguins which live around the coastline. But nothing lives or grows in the frozen interior away from the shore.

As a result the *Discovery* explorers had to carry every scrap of food, fuel and equipment to stay alive for up to two years. Every inch of space on board was used to store supplies.

The decks were covered with boxes, heaps of coal for the ship's boilers, 23 howling sledge dogs and even 45 terrified sheep, who would provide the men with fresh meat on the journey south.

Below decks Tom and the other explorers were jammed together like sardines amidst the jumble of boxes and equipment. There was not enough space for all the men to sleep and as one sailor jumped out of his hammock to report for duty, another would leap into the bed to grab a few hours' sleep.

Discipline on board was very strict. Captain Scott insisted that the seamen should scrub *Discovery's* decks every day, despite the freezing cold. But water tipped onto the wooden decks immediately froze and the sailors needed shovels to break up the solid ice.

Discovery, whose sides had been specially strengthened to withstand the ice, reached the shores of Antarctica after a few weeks and Captain Scott found a suitable bay to moor the ship during the winter months.

Winter in the Antarctic is brutal and travel is mostly impossible.

Discovery arrived in the Antarctic as autumn was approaching and the sudden sharp drop in temperatures shocked the explorers. The thermometer nose dived, the seas froze and ice closed in around *Discovery*. Unable to move, the ship was frozen solid in the ice. Escape was impossible.

The explorers did not have a radio or telephone to contact the outside world and alert rescuers. No ships would pass by and no one was looking for them. The green fields of New Zealand, the nearest civilised land, were 3,200km (2,000 miles) away.

The Antarctic seasons are the opposite of those in Europe's northern regions. April in the south is the equivalent of October in Europe and August is equal to February.

In silence, the explorers were facing the prospect of a bleak Antarctic winter when it is dark for 24 hours a day. The sun dips below the horizon in mid-April and disappears for four months. It reappears in August.

Many hated the idea of constant darkness. Most also knew that some of the first men to endure the gloomy Antarctic winter went mad.

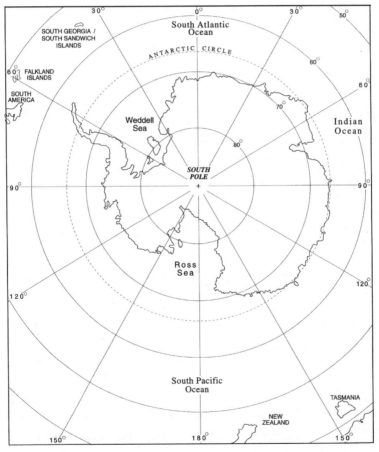

The Antarctic: the fifth largest continent was largely unexplored at the start of the twentieth century.

Chapter 4

LIFE AT THE EXTREMES

Tom Crean was chosen to make the *Discovery* expedition's first sledging expedition into the icy interior on the Antarctic mainland. Tom, who was very proud of his roots, flew the Irish flag on his sledge – the first time the flag had flown in the Antarctic.

It was only a short trip over the ice but it gave the men an early taste of the hazards of exploring in dangerous conditions. The men noticed that temperatures dropped sharply and winds howled more strongly as they moved away from the shore and penetrated inland.

A typical sledging party was made of four or six men, who wore a harness to drag the sledge which carried all their supplies. It was a back-breaking task, particularly when the snow was soft or the ice was slippery.

The sledge carried equipment, like a tent and sleeping bags, plus essential items like food and fuel for cooking. A four-man sledge weighed around 360kg (800lbs), more than the total combined weight of the four men.

Pulling 360kg (800lbs) over the ice was very hard work and it felt like dragging a heavy load over sand or through deep water. The runners on the bottom of the sledge, which look like skis, sometimes froze solidly to the ice and needed a huge effort by the men to jerk the sledge loose.

At night the cold was so severe that the six men packed themselves inside a tent meant only for three, huddled together in sleeping bags. It was very uncomfortable but the warmth of their bodies stopped them freezing.

It was only a short trip and the men were glad to make it safely back to the comfort of the ship. They also warned the others about the dangers when venturing outside.

Men were never far from danger. On one trip, it was so cold the thermometer broke, as the temperature plunged below -50°C (-60°F). One of Tom's friends suffered badly from frostbite in the foot.

The man's foot was like a block of ice and the flesh turned a deathly white. It was vital to warm up the limb. Unless it could be coaxed back to life, the man's foot would have to be cut off.

Someone had a bright idea. Despite the intense cold, the men lifted their jumpers to allow the stricken man to place his foot on their warm stomachs to bring it back to life.

Having an icy foot on their belly was torture for Tom and the others. The man's foot was so bitterly cold that they could only endure the 'cure' for ten minutes at a time. But the plan worked and the lucky sailor's foot slowly came back to life.

Tom was one of the best sledgers on the *Discovery* expedition. He was tough, strong and reliable, and popular with the other explorers.

The expedition spent two years in the Antarctic and during the long stay Tom spent 149 days (over five months) pulling a sledge across the ice and snow, more time than most of the men. Hundreds of miles of new land were discovered, mountains and glaciers were seen for the first time and large gaps in the map were filled in.

One of his comrades said Tom had the 'heart of a lion'. He was brave, loyal and always cheerful. When things went wrong or the weather battered the explorers, it was Tom's joyful optimism which gave other men hope and lifted spirits. He was never downhearted and helped inspire the others to struggle through when all hope seemed lost.

But Tom could do nothing about the trapped ship. The ice refused to loosen its grip around *Discovery* and the explorers faced the threat of abandoning the ship to the mercy of the ice.

Luckily, the navy had sent rescue ships to lift the men off. The explorers were saved, but sailors do not like abandoning a ship. In desperation, dynamite charges were placed in the ice and the explorers began blasting their way to freedom. At first the explosions did not shift the ice and *Discovery* remained stuck fast.

However, one day the ice suddenly began to break up and the ship was freed. The men celebrated and prepared to go home.

Discovery pulled away from the cold wilderness and steamed back to New Zealand's green fields on Good Friday, 1904. It was over two years and three months since Tom had volunteered to step into the unknown.

Chapter 5

THE CALL OF THE ICE

Tom Crean did not delay when he was later asked to return to the frozen Antarctic continent. He simply said yes.

The chance came only a few years later when Captain Scott launched a new expedition, to be the first team to reach the South Pole. He wanted the staunch Tom to sail with him – and perhaps be among the select group of men to stand at the Pole itself.

Hopes were high as the exploration ship, *Terra Nova* – which means 'New Land' – sailed from London in the summer of 1910. People crowded onto the dockside to wave flags and shout their final farewells to the brave men.

Terra Nova sailed around the world to Australia, where the ship picked up enough supplies to keep the men alive for two years. Then the men received a great shock.

The stunning news was that Roald Amundsen, a famous Norwegian explorer, was planning to race Captain Scott to the Pole. Amundsen was a skilled Polar explorer and his fellow Norwegians were experts at travelling across the ice and snow. He was a major threat.

The two exploration ships, Captain Scott's *Terra Nova* and

Amundsen's *Fram*, headed south at the same time, both eager to capture the great prize of being the first to the Pole.

The *Terra Nova* was weighed down with men, piles of food and equipment for at least two years of isolation. More than 30 sledge dogs were chained up in kennels and room was made for a special cargo of nineteen ponies from the cold region of Manchuria in Asia.

Tom took along a big surprise of his own.

Without telling anyone, Tom smuggled a rabbit on board and hid her in the bales of hay which were stacked on deck to feed the ponies. But Tom's secret did not last long. On Christmas Day, Tom's rabbit surprised everyone by giving birth to seventeen babies.

Tom's shipmates all wanted their own rabbit. Tom cheekily promised 22 men they could each have a new pet – though the mother had only seventeen babies. Some of his shipmates were to be very disappointed.

But the expedition came close to disaster on the way south. Hurricane force winds of 120kph (75mph) lashed *Terra Nova* and the men feared they would sink in the very rough seas.

Water poured over the decks and into the holds below. Tom and other sailors formed a human chain with buckets to bail out the floods.

On one occasion a giant wave swept across the decks and hurled one of the sledge dogs into the raging sea. Seconds later another

wave from the other direction carried the helpless dog back on deck. Somehow the dog survived. But two of the ponies died during the furious storm.

Terra Nova survived the hurricane ordeal and finally reached the Antarctic coast, a familiar sight for Tom. The explorers did not want to risk the ship being frozen in again so a wooden hut was built to provide protection from the bitter winter and the ship returned to Australia for the time being.

When the hut was completed the men said goodbye to the ship and knew they would not see *Terra Nova* for at least twelve months. For the second time in his life Tom prepared to endure the pitch black winter months.

The winter isolation meant months confined to the hut and lots of jobs like mending sleeping bags or making sledges. At least it was warm and safe inside.

Going outside was hazardous. There were no lights and the men never strayed more than a few metres from the hut in case they became lost in the swirling blizzards and winter blackness. Guide ropes were strung up between the out-buildings to help men feel their way around.

All they could do was wait for the sun to reappear and think about the race to the Pole.

Chapter 6

THE DASH TO THE POLE

Tom Crean was a vital member of the team bidding to the reach the Pole. He was tough and dependable and had gained valuable knowledge of the snow and ice on his earlier expedition south.

The journey was a huge challenge. From the base camp to the South Pole and back was a trek of 2,800km (1,800 miles) across the worst terrain in the world.

It would take around five months and for most of the time, the explorers would have to drag their own sledges carrying every scrap of food and item of equipment.

To keep the men alive on the round trip to and from the Pole it was necessary to build supply depots along route. Extra teams of men carried these vital supplies of food and fuel, which were dropped off in the snow before the supply parties returned to base camp. The main party, returning from the Pole, would rely on these depots for their food.

The first phase of the journey was a 640km (400 miles) march across the great ice barrier, a flat shelf of ice about the size of France. The shelf is about half a mile thick and to the explorers it was like crossing a vast frozen lake.

Next the party had to climb the mighty Beardmore Glacier, which is 190km (120 miles) long and rises almost 3.2km (2 miles) upwards onto the Polar Plateau.

The final leg was the fearsome Polar Plateau, a distance of around 560km (350 miles) to the Pole itself. The Plateau is roughly 3km (2 miles) above sea level and on this stretch the men faced the worst cold and most powerful winds.

To add to their worries, the air is thinner at these heights and the heavy work of hauling a sledge left the explorers gasping for breath.

On the first leg across the flat ice barrier, the explorers would use the ponies to drag the heaviest sledges. When the ponies became too weak to travel further, the men pulled on their own harness and dragged them.

Tom led a gentle pony called Bones. He loved animals and became very fond of the placid pony. Once during the winter Bones became sick and Tom stayed up all night nursing him back to health.

But ponies are not suited to walking over ice and snow. Their hooves sank deeply into the soft snow, they slipped on the ice and felt bitterly cold. It was a terrible ordeal and the animals suffered badly.

After a few weeks of straining and struggling with the ponies, the explorers had to take a tough decision. The animals were drained and weak. The explorers had no choice but to put the feeble animals out of their misery.

It was an act of mercy to shoot them. The alternative was to watch the ponies freeze or slowly starve to death.

Tom's faithful Bones was among the last to die. Tom was sad, but he knew that Bones would not have survived much longer.

But Bones and the other loyal ponies gave the explorers one important last service – fresh meat, which gave the men enough food and energy to continue their long march.

Not all animals are poor travellers on the ice. Dogs are far better equipped for the task. They are lighter and do not sink into the snow like the heavier ponies. They travel faster than men or ponies and need less food. Carrying less food enabled dog teams to travel longer distances.

A famous explorer was once asked what three things he would take on an Antarctic expedition. He replied: 'Dogs, dogs and more dogs.'

However, Captain Scott did not trust dogs and he struggled to cope with them. He believed dogs were pets, not working animals. His dog teams were kept on the fringe of the expedition and were not used properly.

His rival in the race to the Pole, Amundsen, on the other hand, had great faith in dogs and took 100 animals to haul his sledges. Dogs were central to his plan of attack.

He saw dogs purely as workers and treated them severely. Any dog that grew weak on the journey was immediately shot and fed to the stronger animals.

Without dog teams, Tom and his fellow explorers became like working animals. The men pulled on their harness and dragged the sledges like dogs or ponies.

There were four men in a hauling team and they pulled for around ten hours a day, sometimes longer. The sledge, loaded down with weeks of food supplies and vital equipment, weighed about 360kg (800lbs).

Despite the cold, the hard labour of pulling the sledge over soft snow made the men sweat heavily. But the moisture instantly froze on their bodies, making them feel even colder. The ice then thawed out again because of the hard work and the process started all over again.

Pulling a heavy sledge up the awesome Beardmore Glacier, one of the biggest glaciers in the world, was the hardest part of the journey. The men faced constant danger.

The Beardmore is very slippery and covered in dangerous, hidden crevasses which can easily swallow an entire sledging party.

One of Tom's friends had a close brush with death as they climbed the glacier. The weak ice collapsed under their weight and Tom's pal, Bill Lashly, suddenly disappeared down a gaping hole.

Luckily the sledge was jammed across the hole and he hung helplessly by his harness, spinning over the deep chasm below. A rope was quickly thrown down and Bill was hauled to safety. It was a close shave.

By chance it was Bill's birthday. As Bill scrambled back to his feet, Tom cheerfully wished him 'Happy Birthday!' Bill's reply is unprintable.

Each day the men plodded onwards, looking forward to the evening when they could stop for dinner and a restful night's sleep. A tent was pitched as quickly as possible and small blocks of ice were melted to make a hot drink of cocoa or tea.

The explorers' food was horrible, yet they had no choice but to eat it. There was no alternative.

The basic meal on the march was made from dried meat paste, called pemmican. The paste was mixed with boiling water and dried biscuits which made an unsavoury dish that looked like a thick porridge.

The mix was poured into tin mugs and known as 'hoosh'. It was boring eating the same meal every day so the 'hoosh' was often mixed with curry powder to vary the flavour.

One day Tom was making a hot cocoa drink when he mistook curry powder for cocoa. Without realising his mistake, Tom swallowed the hot curry drink in one gulp without even flinching.

A few mug-fulls of hoosh for breakfast and dinner did not satisfy the hungry men. They finished every meal wishing they had more.

At night they climbed into their fur sleeping bags, tired and longing for a slap up meal. Often they dreamed of giant feasts. But woke to find only another mug full of hoosh and ten hours in the sledging harness.

Chapter 7

TEARDROPS IN THE SNOW

Tom Crean was a tower of strength, power and stamina as the men struggled up the Beardmore Glacier.

Tom hoped that his efforts in the sledging harness would mean that Captain Scott would choose him in the final party of men who were destined to make the last dash to the Pole.

As they climbed up the glacier, Captain Scott had twelve men to choose from. But only four would travel to the Pole. At the top, Captain Scott built a fresh supply depot and sent four men back to base camp, leaving eight still marching onwards.

Spirits were high but not all the men could go the Pole. Some would be disappointed when the next party had to turn back.

The explorers took time off from hauling to celebrate Christmas Day. In two little green tents on the Polar Plateau thousands of miles from civilisation, the eight men settled down to a minor feast.

A special menu was prepared for the day. The hoosh was flavoured with slices of horse meat, doses of curry powder and chunks of onion. A plum pudding was found and the banquet was rounded off with sweets and washed down with piping hot mugs of cocoa.

For a moment, the tiredness and strain were forgotten.

Days later Captain Scott dropped a bombshell. He decided to take five men onto the Pole and send three back to base – including Tom.

Tom was in tears. The Pole was only 240km (150 miles) away, which was a march of about two weeks. The disappointment was awful and Tom felt Captain Scott had let him down.

Tom had served Captain Scott faithfully for ten years. But Captain Scott was a difficult man who did not like quarrels. He expected men like Tom to accept orders without question.

Captain Scott hated the thought of telling Tom he was not going to the Pole. To hide his true feelings, he looked for an excuse.

He went into Tom's tent and prepared to break the bad news. Inside Tom was quietly puffing on his pipe.

As Captain Scott poked his head inside the tent, Tom had been clearing his throat and coughed. It was the excuse Captain Scott wanted.

Captain Scott said, 'You've got a bad cold, Crean'.

Tom was a smart man, and quickly understood the real meaning. He saw right through Captain Scott and snapped back, 'I understand a half-sung song, sir'.

The sharp comment did not change Captain Scott's mind. Tom had to turn round and head back to base camp, while his five colleagues went to the Pole.

It was a bitterly cold day as the parties split. One group was on course to make history, while the other dejected men were going home.

Temperatures fell to -27°C (-17°F) and the sharp wind chilled them to the bone. All the men shook hands and said goodbye.

Standing on the freezing Polar Plateau, the three men returning to camp watched in silence as the five-man sledging party trudged off towards their goal. Slowly the group moved away, getting smaller and smaller as they trudged south. Now and again someone turned and waved.

The dark images of the five men and a sledge stood out clearly against the dazzling white, ice-capped land. Before long the men were just little specks on the vast white horizon. Suddenly they melted into whiteness and were gone.

Tears welled up inside Tom's eyes, then slowly rolled down his cheeks and onto the snow.

It was the last time anyone saw Captain Scott and his men alive.

Chapter 8

A RACE FOR LIFE

Tom Crean turned for home knowing that he faced a different sort of race to Captain Scott's Polar party – Tom faced a race for life.

The journey from the Polar Plateau to base camp was about 1,200km (750 miles). It would take about six or seven weeks, a daunting task for men tired after weeks hauling their sledge so close to the Pole.

Tom was thankful that he had good men alongside him for the long trip. One was his friend, Bill Lashly, who was very tough. Tom and Bill had been together on *Discovery* and both understood the ice.

In charge was Lieutenant Teddy Evans, a good naval officer who knew the dangers ahead. He understood they would be lucky to get back safely.

Lt Evans was critical to their safety. He was the only one with the skills to navigate, which was essential on the Plateau and the flat ice shelf where there were no land features like mountains to guide the men. Tom and Bill would never find their food depots if anything happened to Lt Evans.

Tiredness was a huge factor. Even before they began their march home, the three men were worn out. They had been on the march for almost ten weeks without a break and their meals of hoosh left them hungry.

The sledge, which contained all their life-saving food and camping gear, weighed 180kg (400lbs). For tired, hungry men, it felt a lot heavier.

The fight for life took a bad turn as they began the climb back down the Beardmore Glacier. Food was running dangerously low and they urgently needed to find the next supply depot. There was no time to waste.

But a grim sight awaited the men as they climbed an icy hill and scanned the horizon for a way forward. Ahead lay a jumble of broken ground and dangerous crevasses.

One option was to turn round and re-trace their steps in hopes of finding a safer route. However, food was running low and they could not afford to lose time by going back.

A stark choice faced the desperate explorers. Either waste more time finding a way out of the frozen maze or take a chance. There was no choice.

It was decided to climb aboard the sledge and use it as a toboggan to slide down the icy slope. This was a reckless gamble, but with food running out there was little option.

Quickly the men clambered onto the sledge and wrapped their arms tightly around each other. With a loud yell, Tom, Bill and Lt Evans kicked off and the sledge raced crazily downhill.

The sledge gathered speed as it rocketed downwards, skimming over the slippery surface and jumping across the yawning black crevasses which threatened to swallow them whole.

It was hair-raising. There was no brake on the sledge and no one was sure where they would stop.

The men gripped each other tightly and screamed out loud as the bulky sledge bumped and scraped along the frozen surface. Struggling to hang onto one another, the men were powerless to guide the toboggan as it tumbled without any means of stopping.

The men shrieked as the sledge hurtled downhill at a speed of around 100kph (60mph) – a mixture of sheer terror and excitement.

Without warning the sledge suddenly crashed into an ice ridge, capsized and rolled over and over. The men were tossed around like rag dolls. Finally it came to a stop. They had survived.

Slowly, the three men stood up, shook the snow off themselves and inspected the damage. Amazingly, no one was hurt. They were incredibly lucky to have hit a soft snow bank at the bottom of the slope. A collision with rocks or tumbling over the edge of a crevasse would have been fatal.

The only small casualty of the terrifying ride down the icy slope was Tom's trousers, which were in tatters. It could have been far worse. But the amazing gamble had paid off. The men were very lucky.

Soon after they had another stroke of good fortune when the food depot came into view. That night, the warming meal tasted better than normal. But the danger had not passed.

A few miles further down the giant Beardmore Glacier, the men were again lost in a maze of crevasses and chunky blocks of snow. One gaping crevasse was big enough to have swallowed a mighty cathedral and the men looked for a safe detour around the chasm.

Searching for a way out of the maze, the men spotted a 'bridge' of ice which might offer hope. It looked fragile and beneath was a bottomless black hole. The gamble was whether the 'bridge' could take the weight of three men and a heavy sledge.

Slowly, the men guided the sledge towards the shaky ice bridge. All three were roped together in case someone fell. No one dared to look down. No one spoke.

Bill went across first, moving slowly on all fours. At the other side he called Tom and Lt Evans across. Inch by inch, Tom and the officer guided the sledge across the 'bridge'. Somehow, it withstood the weight, and the men got across.

It was a terrifying moment and Tom later commented, 'We went along the crossbar to the H of Hell'.

Once again, luck was on their side. Soon after, they reached the bottom of the Beardmore Glacier and stumbled across their next precious food depot. Tom let out a yell of joy loud enough to frighten the ponies from their icy grave.

But it was still 640km (400 miles) from base camp. And safety.

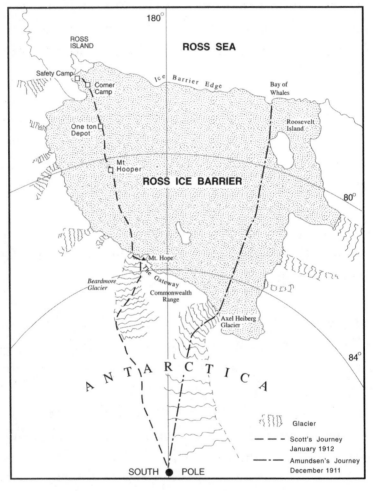

The route to the Pole: Amundsen and Scott's tracks on their 1,800-mile journeys in 1911-12.

Chapter 9

RAW COURAGE

Disaster struck without warning. And where they least expected it.

One morning, Tom Crean and Bill spotted that Lt Evans, the officer, was ill. This was a calamity because Lt Evans was the navigator, and crossing the ice barrier was like crossing an ocean. Crossing an ocean without plotting a course was unthinkable.

Without someone to navigate, there was a serious risk of getting lost and missing the crucial food depots. The food depots were the means of life because the men were only capable of hauling enough food and equipment for about a week at a time.

At best, the explorers hoped that the sledge and ski tracks made on the outward journey might still be visible and offer a pathway home. But the unspoken fear was that the tracks had been covered.

Lt Evans' illness was no ordinary complaint. He had developed the dreaded disease of scurvy. The ailment, which had been the curse of sailors for centuries, is caused by a lack of vitamin C in the body.

Humans normally get their vitamin C from eating fresh fruit, meat or vegetables. In modern times scurvy has almost ceased to exist.

But Tom, Bill and Lt Evans had been on the march without fresh food for almost three months and scurvy was slowly taking a grip. Hoosh was not fresh and contained no Vitamin C.

Lt Evans was the first to crack from the lack of fresh produce. But it was only a matter of time before Tom and Bill would be struck down.

The race for life gathered new urgency. The men marched as fast as their strength allowed. But they were growing more tired and Lt Evans was going rapidly downhill. He barely had strength to pull the sledge and a few days later he collapsed.

It was still a slog of over 320km (200 miles) to the safety of base camp.

Tom and Bill watched in horror as Lt Evans' condition grew steadily worse. He was too ill to pull the sledge and limped alongside, trying not to fall behind. But his strength faded quickly and after a short period Lt Evans broke down completely, unable to walk.

It was 160km (100 miles) to base camp.

Tom knew that Lt Evans was slowly dying. On one occasion Lt Evans fainted. Tears filled Tom's eyes as he knelt down to revive the man. Tom's warm salty tears rolled down his face and dripped onto Lt Evans' face, waking him.

Lt Evans stirred and quickly came to terms with the perilous situation. He knew the terrible truth and mumbled a shocking order to Tom and Bill. 'Leave me behind and save yourselves,' he told the men.

Tom and Bill refused. Navy seamen were taught to obey orders from officers. But Tom and Bill knew the only hope of saving Lt Evans' life was to defy the direct order.

Gently they picked Lt Evans up and placed him on the sledge. They intended to drag him home.

It was an enormous risk. Tom and Bill had been on the march without a break for about fifteen weeks. They were shattered and more and more hungry as each day passed.

With Lt Evans a passenger on the sledge, the tired pair were pulling extra weight. Two men were also dragging a sledge meant for three or four fit and well-fed men.

To ease their load, all gear and equipment not needed was dumped in the snow. Even their skis, which were made of wood and far heavier than today's lightweight models, were thrown out.

Tom and Bill had abandoned everything except the bare necessities. All they had left to give up was their own lives.

The exhausted men dragged the dying Lt Evans along at snail's pace. They pulled the sledge for ten hours a day, covering barely one mile an hour. Each day temperatures began to drop as the warmer, summer climate gave way to the cooler autumn times.

At night they tenderly lifted Lt Evans off the sledge and placed him in his sleeping bag. Lt Evans was so ill that he thought each night would be his last on earth. One night he thought Tom and Bill were lowering him into his grave.

The outlook was grim but Tom never lost hope. Somehow he stayed cheerful and optimistic that the men would pull through. As they put up the tent at the end of the day, Tom sang songs to hearten Bill and Lt Evans.

But Tom's optimism could not cover up a hopeless situation. The strength of Tom and Bill was draining away and the men were not eating enough. Lt Evans was on the brink of death.

A full day's march of ten hours was not good enough to make up the miles needed to get home and their food would run out before they reached safety. Each step came more slowly. Although they spent the same hours marching, they covered less ground.

The impact of biting winds and freezing temperatures hit them harder as each day passed. Hungry people feel the cold more than the well-fed and the crisis for Tom and Bill was not far away.

Nor could they expect rescue from the men at base camp. No one there knew they were in trouble and did not consider it important to send rescue parties. Their fate was in their own hands.

Slowly the party came to within 65km (40 miles) of the hut at base camp. At their current rate of progress, it would be a march of about six to eight days. But there was only enough food for two or three days of travel.

In desperation, the starving men decided to cut the hoosh ration by half. It was another amazing risk. Tom and Bill hoped that by spreading their food over more days it would be possible to march for longer. But cutting down the food for ravenous men was a grave step.

A day later their strength finally ran out as the men camped 56km (35 miles) from the safe haven of base camp. That night Tom and Bill sank to their knees in the snow, gasping for breath at the end of the day's terrible march. They were worn out and unable to take another painful step. They could not drag the sledge another inch.

The men clung to the faint hope that Captain Scott's party of five men, which was returning from the South Pole, might be travelling faster and would catch them up on the way back to base. Or that fast-moving dog teams from base camp might be out on the snow searching for them.

Tom went outside and searched the distant horizon in both directions. He hoped to see little black specks moving slowly towards him, from either direction.

But Captain Scott was not coming. Nor were dogs and rescue parties from base camp.

Tom, Bill and Lt Evans were alone on the ice.

Chapter 10

THE BRAVEST MARCH

Tom Crean gazed at the watch hands as they ticked slowly to 10 o'clock on the morning of Sunday 18 February. It was a bright day – the sun shone and bounced off the ice making him squint against the dazzle. It was freezing, but the wind was mercifully light.

Tom ducked his head into the tent and said goodbye to Lt Evans, lying still in his sleeping bag. He shook hands with Bill.

Seconds later Tom began the most daring escapade of his life – a bold attempt to reach base camp alone and fetch rescuers for the dying Lt Evans and his friend, Bill. It was a life or death decision.

That morning it was agreed that Tom and Bill could not possibly drag the sledge any further. But they would die if they stayed in the tent. So Tom bravely volunteered to walk 56km (35 miles) to the base hut alone.

Tom was not a man to shirk a challenge. But he also knew this was a formidable task and if he failed it was certain death for Bill and Lt Evans. Tom also faced his own death if he broke a leg on the ice or fell down a crevasse.

Tom was in no fit state to make such a tiring journey.

He was dreadfully tired and gaunt, having walked about 2,400km (1,500 miles) in the previous four months. He was bitterly cold and ravenously hungry. It was many days since he last felt the joy of a full stomach.

Nor was he equipped for the march. Tom decided not to take his heavy sleeping bag and there was only one tent and portable stove to make hot food and drinks. Bill would need these to nurse the fading Lt Evans.

Nor did Tom have enough food for the journey. Little remained to keep him alive on his heroic walk. A quick survey of the few remaining rations came up with just three biscuits and two sticks of chocolate.

Tom stumbled into the unknown, determined to cover the distance as fast as possible. But even a cheerful optimist like Tom must have doubted his chances of surviving in the hostile, frozen wilderness on so little food and without a tent or sleeping bag.

Tom set off, trudging slowly and sinking up to his thighs in the soft snow. Snow shoes or skis might have helped but they had been ditched miles back on the march to save weight. He was on his own.

Today's explorers wear crampons with metal spikes that provide a grip on the glassy ice. But Tom's fur boots had flat smooth soles which gave no grip and he often slipped over. He would be very lucky not to injure himself.

It was freezing. The winds, although fairly light, whipped up small ice fragments and cut into Tom's face as he set out. To combat the ice, he held his arm up against his face as a protective shield.

In the tent Bill propped up the feeble Lt Evans. Together they watched in silence as Tom plodded wearily through the banks of soft snow or slithered over the slippery ice. He was the only dark object visible on the white wasteland. A hopeful speck.

Tom struggled on, occasionally looking back to see the little tent he had left behind. But he was confident that he could conquer the ice.

Progress was painfully slow. He was terribly tired and hunger gnawed away at his stomach. His only drink was an occasional handful of ice scooped off the ground. He longed for a warming mug of steaming hot tea or coffee.

Tom stumbled, crawled and walked for hours without taking a break. He covered sixteen miles, almost half the distance to the hut, before pausing for a rest.

Panting for breath, he sat down in the snow and ate two biscuits and the two sticks of chocolate. He craved a hot drink. Tom placed the last biscuit back in his pocket – for emergencies!

Taking a break did not help Tom. It made him feel tired. But dozing off to sleep was too risky in the cold. He would freeze to death.

So he hurriedly started to walk again. All around were treacherous crevasses that could gobble up a man in a moment. He could not relax or afford to take a wrong step.

Slowly, but surely, Tom edged towards base camp. After a few more hours he came to a small hill near the hut. From the hilltop he would be able to look down on the hut and perhaps call for help.

But the climb was a terrible ordeal. Normally he might have run up the hill. However, Tom was so exhausted that he hardy walk straight and at times he crawled on all fours.

Finally he made it up the hill, but a huge blow waited at the summit. Tom looked down on the hut and strained his eyes to catch signs of men or dogs moving about below. But there was nothing.

The sight shattered Tom. It meant there was no one in the hut to fetch rescue for Bill and Lt Evans. Without help, Tom would be forced to try and reach the expedition's other hut, which was a further 22km (14 miles) away across the ice. The thought of another march was terrible.

To hide the awful disappointment, Tom ate his last biscuit and sucked on a bit of ice. But over his shoulder a new menace was threatening.

From the hill, Tom could see darkening clouds in the distance which signalled that a blizzard was blowing in his direction. He noticed that the wind had picked up and he felt much colder. Nobody could survive a ferocious Antarctic blizzard in the open – not even Tom.

He scurried down the hill as best he could, puffing for breath. Sometimes he fell heavily. In the distance, the roaring, pitiless blizzard was racing towards him.

Tom was now desperate. The race for life had entered the final lap and the brutal Antarctic weather closed in for the kill.

He was given fresh hope though, as he crept nearer the hut. Looking down in the snow he saw a scattering of paw prints from the dog teams. It was the signs of life he craved.

The sight injected new life into his frail body and Tom hurried forward towards the hut, determined to win the race against the fearsome blizzard.

Calling on the final reserves of strength and resolve, Tom staggered to the door. He took a faltering step inside and collapsed on the floor, delirious with hunger and exhaustion, and numbed with the cold.

By an amazing stroke of luck, one of the two men inside the hut that day was a doctor – the only doctor within 640km (400 miles).

He quickly gave Tom a tot of brandy to revive him. Tom gulped it down and was promptly sick. Outside, the deadly blizzard struck the hut like a hammer blow. A few more minutes outside and Tom would have died.

It was 3.30 on the morning of Monday 19 February. Tom's incredible solo march of 56km (35 miles) had taken almost eighteen hours, without proper rest, hot food or drink.

Tom, a modest man, did not boast about his remarkable act of bravery. He simply said, 'My long legs did the trick. But I must say I was pretty well done for when I finished'.

It was the greatest act of single-handed bravery in the entire era of early Polar exploration.

Chapter 11

LIFE AND DEATH ON THE ICE

Tom Crean was in an appalling state after his astonishing solo march to save Bill and Lt Evans. But it did not dent his courage. He bravely volunteered to climb off his sickbed and return to the ice to rescue his colleagues.

The doctor refused to let him go. He waited for the blizzard to blow itself out and instead took a team of fast-moving husky dogs to locate the little tent where Bill and Lt Evans waited patiently. They were just in time.

The dogs galloped to the tent door barking loudly. One stuck his head through the tent flap and licked Lt Evans' face. He was barely alive.

Tom was reunited with his companions at the hut. Bill and Lt Evans had survived an appalling ordeal only because of the raw courage and single-handed bravery of Tom.

It was an outstanding act of heroism and Tom was later rewarded with the Albert Medal, the highest award for gallantry. King George V pinned the medal on Tom's chest at a special ceremony at Buckingham Palace, London, on his return from the Antarctic.

The dreadful state of Tom, Bill and Lt Evans set alarm bells ringing at base camp. The explorers there now worried about the fitness of Captain Scott's party on the way back from the South Pole. If tough characters like Tom were in trouble, Captain's Scott must be struggling, too.

Some feared the worst. And sadly, they were right.

Captain Scott and his four companions reached the South Pole in January 1912, only a few weeks after separating from Tom on the Polar Plateau. But they arrived to discover dog tracks and the Norwegian flag flapping in the wind. Amundsen had won the race to the Pole by just one month.

Captain Scott's group were bitterly disappointed and freezing cold. The 1,400km (900 miles) return journey was another race for life. Tragically all five men died on the trek back.

In the safety and warmth of base camp hut, the men waited for the Polar party to walk through the door. Every noise from outside the hut was thought to be the returning explorers. On clear days they climbed the hill outside the hut and looked towards the distant horizon in the hope of seeing small dark objects moving slowly towards them. But the five men never appeared.

Months passed and it was clear that Captain Scott's Polar party was dead. All that remained was to sit through another dark Antarctic winter and wait for the spring before launching another trip to the ice to search for the bodies.

Tom had recovered from his ordeal during the winter months and once again he trekked south, in search of the Polar team. After a few weeks travel a small dark object caught their attention. It was the tip of Captain Scott's dark green tent poking out from a mound of snow.

The men scraped the snow off the tent. Inside they found the bodies of Captain Scott and two colleagues. Two others had died on the march and their bodies were never found.

The men were devastated. Tom was in tears when he bent down and gently kissed Captain Scott's forehead.

The tent was collapsed over the bodies and a huge mound of snow was built into a mighty cairn to cover the dead men. All stood in silence. Temperatures had plunged to -29° (-20°) and the icy wind stung their faces.

It was time to go home. The expedition ship, *Terra Nova*, returned to base camp during the summer and picked up the survivors. Months later they were back in Europe. The expedition party had been gone for over two years.

Chapter 12

ICE BOUND

The call of the ice was strong for Tom Crean. Within eighteen months of burying Captain Scott, Tom headed back to the Antarctic.

He was now one of the most experienced explorers of the ice age and the famous Sir Ernest Shackleton asked him to go south again. Shackleton had travelled with Tom on the *Discovery* expedition and wanted his tough, resolute character to join his next undertaking.

Shackleton's new expedition was the most ambitious Antarctic venture ever attempted. His proposal was to walk from coast to coast across the entire continent – a trek of about 2,800km (1,800 miles).

Most of the interior of Antarctica was still unknown and it was a perilous venture. A newspaper advertisement of the time summed up the risks of Polar exploration at the time.

The advertisement read: 'Men wanted for hazardous journey. Small wages, bitter cold, long months of complete darkness, constant danger, safe return doubtful.'

The wages for exploration were small, despite the hazards. Tom was only paid about £3 a week, which is worth around €210 (£145) a week in today's money.

The expedition began in the summer of 1914, as the First World War was breaking out in Europe. Shackleton's ice ship, *Endurance*, intended to sail for the Falkland Islands in the South Atlantic Ocean. But German warships were gathering for a big naval battle so the explorers gave the islands a wide berth.

To avoid trouble, *Endurance* sailed onto the small island of South Georgia on the edge of the Southern Ocean. Other bad news of a different kind awaited them.

South Georgia was a bustling island full of whaling ships and hardened Norwegian sailors with a thorough knowledge of the icy waters off the Antarctic coast. To reach the Antarctic mainland, *Endurance* had to cross 1,600km (1,000 miles) of the treacherous Weddell Sea, which is teeming with giant icebergs and even today poses a huge threat to shipping. Few ships enter the Weddell.

The Norwegian whalers urged the explorers on *Endurance* not to venture into the Weddell Sea that year because the ice was thicker than normal. The ship, the whalers grimly warned, risked getting trapped in the ice and being crushed.

But the advice of the whalers was ignored and *Endurance* sailed.

Endurance ran into serious trouble only weeks after entering the icy waters. With the words of the whalers still ringing in their ears, the explorers watched as the ice closed around the ship. One by one,

the exit routes to open sea lanes were closed off as the ice gathered around and tightened its grip.

Only luck could save them, but the explorers' luck had run out. High winds drove the pack ice closer together and blocked off all exits. *Endurance* was trapped, surrounded on all sides by ice.

As far as the eye could see there was miles of unbroken ice. Old sailors on board remembered the saying, 'What the ice gets, the ice keeps'.

There were 28 men on board the trapped *Endurance*. They were explorers, scientists and some sailors, who had only signed up for a quick round trip to the Antarctic mainland and back.

One man secretly stowed away, and was only discovered a few days after *Endurance* left South Georgia.

The 28 men were trapped together, surrounded by an ocean of ice. There was no radio on board and no ships passed by this hostile, barren region.

They were castaways, cut off from the rest of the world. And the bleak, dark Antarctic winter was approaching.

Chapter 13

TRAPPED

Tom Crean knew what to expect from the sinister Antarctic winter. He was one of the few men on board who had endured the darkness of winters in the south away from the civilised world.

But this was different from his previous trips. *Discovery* was trapped by the ice a few years earlier but the navy knew where the ship was located and was ready to send rescue ships if the explorers could not break free.

Endurance was now trapped, but there were no plans to send rescue ships. Nor was there any guarantee the vessel would escape the ice when the sun returned in the spring. The men from *Endurance* were on their own.

To pass the time, waiting for the ice to break up, the men carried on their research and experiments. Others continued preparations for the Antarctic crossing, still hopeful.

Time moved slowly. Some played football on the ice in gloomy half light before the sun completely disappeared. Others hunted for food, killing seals or penguins. At night they played cards or had a sing-song. In a fit of boredom one day, the 28 men agreed to have their heads shaved.

Attempts were made to break up the ice which had trapped the ship. The men worked for hours, smashing the ice with picks and even using huge saws to cut their way through. But in spite of strenuous work, the ice refused to let go and the ship remained held firmly.

Tom had two special tasks. He was kept busy preparing supplies for the planned overland journey, and looking after his team of sledge dogs.

Tom loved handling the dogs. The leader of Tom's pack was named Surly, who was generally friendly but shocked him once by biting him on the arm. Some of the other dogs were called Samson, Wolf, Shakespeare, Judge, Steamer, Jerry, Saint and Sadie.

Another pet was the ship's cat, who was called Mrs Chippy even though it was a boy. Mrs Chippy was a big favourite with all the men.

The men on board *Endurance* became fond of their animals, often taking photographs of them or feeding them scraps of food from their own plates. The animals were a welcome distraction from the worry of being marooned.

Exercising the dogs was an essential part of the daily routine for Tom and the other dog handlers. It was important to keep the dogs fit and ready to haul sledges when the expedition finally got underway.

Once they organised a special race between six teams of dogs which they called the 'Antarctic Derby'. It was a tough race and Tom's team came third.

Tom received a surprise one day when Sally, one of his favourite dogs, gave birth to four puppies. Tom immediately adopted the pups and named them Roger, Toby, Nell and Nelson.

Tom looked after the puppies well. The dogs loved him and would howl and whine if he left their sight. He built a special home on the ice for the pups, which looked like a small igloo. He called it a 'dogloo'.

Tom trained the dogs to wear a harness and pull a sledge when they were only a few months old. It was vital they learned how to work because there was no place on a Polar expedition for any man or animal who could not work or pull their weight. There was only food for the strong working animals.

Tom taught the dogs to obey orders. The instructions to the pups were simple. He would shout 'Mush' to start the team moving. 'Ha' meant turn left and 'Gee' ordered the dogs to turn right. The command for stop was 'Whoa'.

However, the distraction the dogs provided could not conceal the danger which the men faced.

Food was the main concern. The men had plenty of hoosh and tinned food. But they needed fresh meat to stave off the effects of scurvy and the best hunters in the party went out onto the ice searching for seals or penguins to build up stocks of meat for the winter months when wildlife would mostly disappear.

Seals were especially valuable because they carry blubber fat to keep them warm when swimming in the freezing Antarctic waters. When melted down, the blubber provided fuel for the cooking stoves and lighting lamps.

Any food was welcome. On one occasion, a 3m (10ft) sea leopard climbed onto the ice and tried to attack one of the sailors. The massive beast was shot and made ready for dinner. When the creature was cut open the chef found seven whole but undigested fish inside its stomach. That night the men also had 'fresh' fish for dinner.

The daily diet of fresh seal or penguin meat, which contains the necessary vitamin C, prevented them getting scurvy. But it had another unpleasant side effect. All the men became horribly constipated and were constantly breaking wind.

Wind of a different sort was needed to break up the ice and free the ship. Weeks passed into months and still the ship remained in its unyielding grip.

Although the ship was stuck fast, the ice itself was on the move, drifting slowly along with the currents of the Weddell Sea. The trapped *Endurance* drifted hundreds of kilometres with the flowing currents, but it could not break free.

First the *Endurance* drifted southwards towards the coast of Antarctica where the ship was originally intended to land. The ship drifted so close to shore that the men could see the distant mountains, near where they planned to make their base camp. But miles of ice still lay between the *Endurance* and the shore.

A little later the currents changed direction and turned from south to north. *Endurance* was carried along with the flow and moved away from the land. The mountains disappeared over the horizon.

With the drift to the north went any hope of landing and the expedition making the historic coast-to-coast crossing of the continent. Tom's sledges, which were packed for the crossing, would be needed for a different task.

Endurance was at the mercy of the currents and carried along for about nine months, still locked in the ice and unable to move. The currents carried the ship almost 1,600km (1,000 miles) to the north, away from the coast where they wanted to land but closer and closer towards a greater danger.

Stronger currents began to disturb the ice as the ship moved slowly north into slightly warmer waters. Massive ice blocks began to grind against each other as the currents pushed the ship towards the land hundreds of kilometres away.

The grinding ice pressure posed a major threat to *Endurance.* The wooden ship faced being crushed. Unless the ship could break free into open water, the explorers would have to consider abandoning it and making a dash across the ice to land.

But the nearest land was at least 400km (250 miles) away across broken ice. Only desperate men would even consider such a trip.

Endurance was in grave danger though, and the journey over the ice might be the only way to get home. As the weeks passed, the mounting pressure from the ice began to crush the ship.

The men lay in their beds listening to the sounds of the pressure building up against the ship. The timbers strained and heaved. The only noises in the Antarctic night were the groans of *Endurance* struggling to survive.

However, *Endurance* was losing the battle. The ice began to move more strongly, lifting the ship and tipping it over at an angle. *Endurance* was doomed.

Over the next few weeks the ship's planks split like matchsticks and water poured in. The timbers screeched under the strain. Beams buckled and snapped. The noise was quite eerie.

The men began pumping out the incoming water.

But Tom began packing his sledges with food and equipment. He knew the ship was going to sink.

Chapter 14

CAST ADRIFT

Tom Crean worked frantically. Vital food and supplies were taken off the ship and stored on the ice. The sledges were prepared for a trek. Finding land was now crucial if *Endurance* was lost.

More 'dogloos' were built and the three small lifeboats were carefully taken off the dying ship and perched on the ice. These might be needed if the ice broke up and open lanes of water appeared.

On the ice, the men huddled together, watching the dying agonies of *Endurance*. Around them was an untidy jumble of food, tents, equipment, 60 barking dogs, a small cat and three lifeboats.

The ice-floe, the new floating home for the *Endurance* expedition, was about 2m (6ft) thick. Beneath the floe was 3.5km (2 miles) of black, freezing ocean.

Endurance finally gave up the struggle and sank in November 1915, less than a year after it left South Georgia. Since becoming trapped in the ice, the ship had drifted almost 200km (1,200 miles) in a giant semi-circle around the Weddell Sea.

There were only two possibilities for the 28 castaways.

One was a hazardous trip over the ice to land about 400km (250 miles) away. The other was that the powerful currents of the Weddell Sea would carry their ice-floe further north into warmer waters. At this point the men would pack their lifeboats and sail to land and await rescue. Both were slim, forlorn hopes.

Weeks passed. The ice-floe continued to drift slowly north but there was no sign of open water. The hunters continued to search for fresh stocks of seal and penguin meat. Tom readied his sledges.

It was decided to take a chance and try to reach firm land or open water. Tons of supplies would be needed for the journey and the plan was to place ski runners underneath the lifeboats and drag them over the ice.

Only essential food supplies and vital equipment like tents and cooking materials could be carried on the journey. Everything else was ditched. It was crucial to cut down the weight.

Each man was allowed to keep only 900gm (2lbs) of personal items. Men left gold coins, watches and even a Bible in the snow.

It was also necessary to be ruthless with the animals. Only those who pulled their weight could be taken on the long journey. It was no time for sentiment.

The decision was heartbreaking for Tom. Three of the puppies he had looked after since birth were taken aside and shot. Mrs Chippy, the ship's pet cat, was also shot because the other dogs, who were likely to grow hungry on the march, might attack him.

Even the toughest of explorers had tears in their eyes at the loss of their faithful friends. It was the expedition's saddest day. But it was also an act of mercy for the poor animals.

However, the task of marching to land was hopeless from the start. Shedding the extra weight did not help their cause. The boats were far too heavy to drag. One weighed over 1,000kg (1 ton) and could only be moved with huge effort which drained the men.

Four men went ahead with picks and shovels, clearing a smooth path for the boat-haulers. Behind came fifteen men dragging the heaviest boat and alongside them teams of dogs pulled Tom's sledges. The long train of men, dogs, boats and sledges stretched for almost 800m (½ a mile) across the icy wastes.

The effort was pointless. To their horror, the men discovered that they had travelled only 1.6km (1 mile), in the first day. The next brought another terrible struggle and only another 1.6km (1 mile) of progress. Next day the march was abandoned.

The northward drift of their ice-floe was now their only hope. On its present course, the floe would probably drift close enough to land to risk another slog across the ice.

But if the current changed course, they would drift away from the land, into the vast open seas of the South Atlantic Ocean between the continents of South America and Africa.

The floe drifted further north and shortly before Christmas, the hauling parties gathered again. Another attempt was made to reach land or the open seas.

But the work was harder than ever. The boat's ski runners often became frozen to the ice. At best, the men could only pull about 200m (220 yards) before collapsing exhausted. But by the end of a back-breaking day the party still managed to cover barely 1.6km (1 mile).

The nearest land was reckoned to be around 480km (300 miles) to the west. But at the current rate it would take 10 months of constant toil to reach land. Impossible.

Once again the boat-hauling march was abandoned and the men built a new camp on the ice, watching carefully to see which way the currents took their floe. They called their new home Patience Camp.

A new danger was looming. Food supplies were starting to run low and there was fuel to make only one hot drink a day. In desperation, the men were forced eat dog food.

The run-down of food stocks was bad news for the remaining dogs. Without food the animals would starve to death or suffer brutal attacks from each other. The dogs themselves were also a valuable source of meat for the men. So it was decided to put the animals out of their misery and shoot them. Even Tom's last puppy could not be saved.

Tough men like Tom were in tears. But there was simply no choice.

Only the strongest can survive a Polar expedition.

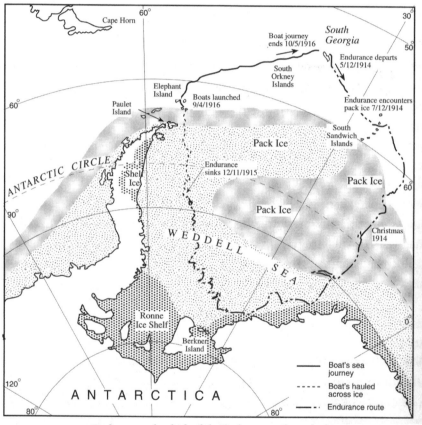

Endurance: the drift of the Endurance *through the Weddell Sea and the expedition's subsequent journeys to Elephant Island and South Georgia.*

Chapter 15

LAUNCH THE BOATS!

Tom Crean swallowed his hot cocoa. It tasted good, warming and refreshing. It was also the last of the cocoa.

Food supplies had fallen to an alarming level. Seals and penguins had mostly disappeared from the ice and men scrabbled round in the snow to retrieve scraps of bones or bits of rotting flesh. Anything was better than nothing.

Most of the tea was gone and the only hot drink was powdered milk laced with sugar.

Just when the castaways needed some good news they felt a slight swell of the sea beneath their feet. A moving sea indicated open water, free from the ice. A glance into the distance showed ice was breaking up. On a clear day, the tips of snow-capped mountains could be seen on the far-off horizon.

But their hopes were soon dashed. The currents took them beyond the distant mountains. They had passed the only known land in the region and were drifting towards open seas and the fearsome Drake Passage, a hostile stretch of water between South America and the Antarctic.

Drifting into the Drake Passage was highly dangerous. The only choice was to search for two tiny islands which lay directly ahead in the path of the current.

But the two specks of land, Clarence Island and Elephant Island, were remote dots in a vast ocean. No one lived on them and no ships passed by.

A further problem was the sharp fall in temperature. It was getting colder as the summer gave way to the autumn season. Winds grew stronger and the days became shorter. No one dared consider another winter on the ice-floe.

Luckily, open stretches of water began to appear as the floe drifted further north. Then the mountain peaks of Clarence and Elephant Island came into view. It was time to launch the boats.

Since entering the ice, the *Endurance* party had travelled about 3,200km (2,000 miles) in a giant semi-circle around the Weddell Sea. No one had been lost. Yet no one realised that the hardest part of the journey still lay ahead.

The three boats, packed with men and supplies, pulled away from Patience Camp. The largest was called the *James Caird* and the next *Dudley Docker*. Tom took charge of the smallest and most vulnerable vessel, the *Stancomb Wills*.

The *Wills*, a tiny craft only 6.3m (20ft) long, carried eight men plus supplies. Everyone rowed, except Tom who steered the little boat between giant chunks of ice which littered the ocean. High winds whipped up the seas and the men were soaked by constant spray.

The target was Elephant Island. It was uninhabited and rocky. But it was dry land.

Dodging icebergs was a constant battle and travel at night was too dangerous. The boats were tied to a berg and the men cooked hoosh and unpacked their sleeping bags on the ice for a well-earned rest.

One night the ice-floe suddenly split open and one sailor was tossed into the sea. When he was pulled out of the water, the sailor's only concern was that his precious tobacco had got wet! But there were no dry clothes for the man so volunteers marched him up and down the ice all night to prevent him freezing to death in the sub-zero temperatures.

The boat journey to Elephant Island, about 160km (100 miles) away, was an easy trip in gentle seas. But it was very risky in the vicious and icy waters of the Southern Ocean.

Tom needed all his experience as a seaman to keep the *Stancomb Wills* afloat in the rough seas. Any collision with the ice would have been fatal but somehow he managed to dodge the threat.

It was also important to keep up the mens' spirits. Tom, standing at the tiller, often cracked a few jokes and sang songs.

The men spent seven terrible days in the boats. They were freezing cold, very tired from rowing and constantly wet. The spray froze to their faces and clothes.

Even going to the toilet was tricky. To relieve themselves men had to dangle their backsides over the side of the swaying boat and expose themselves to freezing cold sea spray. When asked how men went to the toilet on board, the answer was, 'Quickly'.

Some of the men in Tom's boat were suffering badly from the cold and exposure. The temperatures fell to -20°C (-4°F) and the winds whistled to gale force. One sailor, the man who had stowed away, developed severe frostbite in his feet and it was feared others might not survive many more turbulent days in the open boats.

But spirits rose after seven days when the rocky mountains of Elephant Island loomed out of the dark grey clouds. Dry land at last.

Tom steered the little *Stancomb Wills* towards the island. The heavy black mountains and steep cliffs loomed over them. After a hasty search a suitable beach was found. It would make an ideal landing place.

The biggest hurdle was a reef of rocks which jutted out from the sea, blocking their entrance to the safe refuge of the beach. Getting smashed to pieces when so near to safety would be a cruel fate.

The *Wills* moved up and down, anxiously searching for a gap in the reef. Finally an opening was spotted and the little boat was pulled into position. It was pointed towards the thin channel and the men waited for the next incoming wave.

In an instant, the wave broke behind them, carrying the *Stancomb Wills* through the narrow gap. The boat surged towards the shore and came grinding to a noisy halt on the pebble beach.

It was the first time anyone had ever landed on Elephant Island. The last time Tom and the men from *Endurance* had stood on firm land was 497 days ago – one year, four months and three weeks.

Chapter 16

A FRAGILE GRIP ON LIFE

The castaways tottered about like drunks on rubbery legs when they first set foot on Elephant Island. After so long at sea and floating on the ice, solid ground felt strange. Some fell on their knees to give thanks for surviving the terrible journey. Some cried with relief.

Tom Crean shone like a beacon among the wreckage. Many men had suffered badly in the boats. Frostbite and hunger left many weak. But Tom was still strong, helped by his experience of coping with the extremes on the *Discovery* and *Terra Nova* expeditions.

A hot drink of powdered milk was quickly brewed. It had an immediate warming effect and gave the stranded men a moment to consider their fate.

Elephant Island is no place to be marooned. The island offered the castaways only a fragile grip on life.

The steep cliffs and bleak mountains are forbidding and uninviting. Moving inland was not possible. Their narrow beach was exposed to the full rage of the Southern Ocean.

The wind gusted so strongly that big men were blown off their feet.

In haste, two of the lifeboats, the *Dudley Docker* and *Stancomb Wills*, were upturned and the men sheltered underneath from the battering. It was only a minor relief.

The key questions were whether it was possible to survive on the island, and how soon could they get off.

The nearest land to Elephant Island is 1,000km (600 miles) away and they could not hope to be seen by passing ships. Elephant Island was only discovered when a ship was blown off course in a violent storm and no vessels operated in the area. They would have to rescue themselves by sailing to the nearest inhabited region.

The best chance of rescue lay at South Georgia, the island where the *Endurance* expedition began, eighteen months earlier. The whalers on South Georgia worked all year round and could be relied upon to help.

As the crow flies, South Africa or the Falkland Islands were much nearer to the island. But it was impossible to sail against the powerful currents in a small boat and South Georgia was the only sensible choice.

Sailing to South Georgia was a journey of almost 1,300km (800 miles) across the Southern Ocean, the wildest, most violent sea on earth.

Even today's sailors, with modern equipment and specially strengthened ships fear the Southern Ocean. Hurricane winds can screech to 240kph (150mph) and mountainous waves build to 15m (50ft) tall – about the size of a two-storey house.

But not all the men would survive a journey to South Georgia. The weakest were in no fit state and some would die in the attempt. Only the strongest would endure the trip.

It was decided that six men would sail the largest of the three boats – the *James Caird* – to get help from the whalers at South Georgia. The other 22 would stay behind on Elephant Island's rocky beach, camped under the *Dudley Docker* and *Stancomb Wills*.

No one knew how long it would take to reach South Georgia because no one had ever attempted the voyage before. Nor did anyone know which group of men was worse off – those sailing across the harsh Southern Ocean or those clinging to life on the beach.

The epic ocean crossing called for a special breed of man. Only the very toughest and most experienced of sailors had even a remote chance of getting through.

Tom Crean, who had never been afraid to take a step into the unknown, literally begged to make the ocean crossing. At first the leader, Shackleton wanted Tom to remain on Elephant Island to help the castaways. But he soon realised that Tom's seafaring skills and ability to battle against hardship would be vital.

There was no time to waste. The dark Antarctic winter was

approaching and all hands scrambled to make the boat ready.

First, the mast from Tom's boat, the *Stancomb Wills*, was cut down and jammed into the hull of the *James Caird* to provide extra strength. At the same time, planks were stripped from the *Dudley Docker* and used to raise the sides of the *Caird* in the hope of stopping the seas crashing over the top.

A sail was made from spare canvas and next a covering was needed to protect the open boat against the seas. Lids from wooden food cases and odd strips of canvas were used to construct a makeshift decking.

It was tough work. The canvas was frozen stiff in the icy cold and had to be thawed over the burning blubber stove to be workable.

Other men filled canvas food bags with rocks and stones from the beach for ballast which would help keep the little craft steady in the rolling seas. The food, which included normal hoosh, biscuits, powdered milk and some sugar, was loaded aboard and barrels of fresh drinking water were filled.

The 22 men on the beach at Elephant Island were a sorry looking sight as they waved a hearty farewell to the six men facing the hazardous sea journey. 'Hurry back,' they called. The voyage of the *James Caird* was their only hope of survival.

Slowly the boat pulled away from the beach battling against the crashing waves. Occasionally the men waved back.

Large dark waves often blocked their view of the small craft as it moved further from the beach. A little later it re-emerged. Then, suddenly, it was gone.

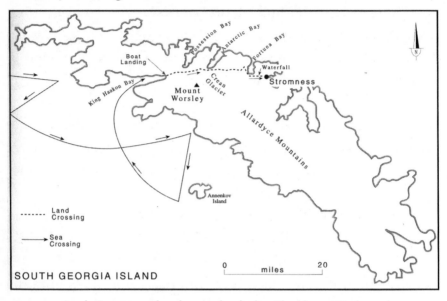

South Georgia was largely unexplored when Shackleton, Worsley and Tom Crean marched across the mountainous, glacier-strewn island in 1916. The map shows the path taken by the James Caird *approaching the island and the route across the island.*

Chapter 17

AN EPIC VOYAGE

Winds hurtled to nearly 50kph (30mph) as the *James Caird* picked its way through the breakers and ice-bergs surrounding Elephant Island. The sky was darkening as evening approached and the only visible light on the ocean was the red glow of Tom Crean's pipe.

The *James Caird* was pitifully small for the risky trip. The boat was only 7m (23ft) long and not designed to cross stormy oceans. With six large men on board, it was very crowded and uncomfortable.

Sleeping bags had to be spread over the tons of small rocks which provided ballast on the bottom of the craft. Each man had his own sleeping bag yet it was difficult to sleep on hard rocks. As a result, three of the bags were spread out over the rocks as a makeshift mattress and the six men shared the remaining three for sleep.

They wore woollen long johns as underwear, shirts, sweaters, trousers and overalls, plus two pairs of socks and woollen mittens. Their boots were made from reindeer skin, but were not waterproof.

The men were soaked to the skin from the constant sea spray and often frostbitten from the biting cold. Small saltwater boils began to appear on their skin. Some lost all feeling in their wet feet which turned a sickly white colour.

Their routine was to have three men up top sailing the boat while below three others tried to snatch some sleep.

Freezing water poured into the boat with every wave and they took turns pumping it out. However, the cold was so severe that a man could only hold his hand under water on the brass cylinder pump for five minutes before it went numb.

Tom was often the cook and he suffered a terrible ordeal at meal times. In the rising and plunging seas, Tom was hunched over the primus stove because there was not enough room to sit upright. Another man pinned him against the side of the boat to ensure he did not fall over in the rolling seas and spill the precious contents of the pot.

There was little comfort on board. The sleeping bags were beginning to fall apart after months of wear and tear and loose hairs from the reindeer fur with which they were made fell everywhere and often floated into the cooking pot.

Once Tom stuck his blackened hand into the pot to fish out a bunch of offending hairs. He squeezed the hair over the pot to make sure that not a drop of the prized hoosh was wasted.

Tom often burnt his hands on the scorching pot. When ready, he quickly filled each man's mug to the brim. It was scoffed down, burning hot, and the first to finish leapt up to replace the man steering the boat.

Meals were washed down with mugs of boiling milk which the men learned to drink far hotter than normal.

However, the constant swell inevitably caused distress for all the men, who became queasy as the boat was tossed around like a cork. Even tough, experienced sailors like Tom were seasick.

Tom was a tower of strength on the *James Caird* though. He never lost his sense of humour or his confidence that the men would reach South Georgia safely. His constant cheerfulness was an important factor in giving the men some hope that they would survive the voyage.

But the toughest job on board the *James Caird* was navigating the vessel to the island. This task fell to Captain Frank Worsley, the captain of *Endurance*, who was known as Skipper.

Even a small margin of error in the Skipper's navigation would send the *James Caird* sailing past the little island and out into the South Atlantic Ocean – the countless thousands of kilometres of open water between the continents of Africa and South America.

If the *Caird* missed South Georgia there was no way of fighting back to land against the strong currents. Skipper had only one chance to find the island. But the boat's safety was threatened by different dangers.

Dawn broke one morning to find thick ice had formed on the *Caird's* canvas decking during the cold night. Sea spray froze as soon as it splashed across the deck. By morning the ice was 15 cm (6 inches) thick and threatened to capsize the boat under its weight.

Urgent action was needed and Tom bravely volunteered to crawl out along the canvas decking to chip away at the ice. As he crawled along on his stomach, the boat rolled heavily and he was almost thrown into the water.

Tom clung to the decking with one hand and knocked off the ice with the other. But he could only hang on for a short while in the freezing temperatures and other members of the crew inched forward and took his place.

It was a thankless task. No sooner had they chipped away at the ice than fresh spray splashed over the deck and immediately froze on the canvas once more.

It was a constant battle and the men risked their lives by crawling out onto the deck to break off the ice. Luckily their efforts worked and the *Caird* had survived a terrible fright.

Another crisis arose soon after. In the distance someone noticed a white cloud low on the horizon and they thought the sky was brightening.

Suddenly it was noticed that the bright cloud was moving towards them. It was a giant wave.

'For God's sake, hold on,' someone shouted.

The *James Caird* was catapulted forward and almost lifted bodily out of the sea as the giant wave crashed down upon the vessel. The men were thrown to the floor and water engulfed them. The men were so wet that for a moment, it was not clear whether the boat was still upright.

But the giant wave disappeared as quickly as it came. The *James Caird* had survived, somehow.

Vast amounts of water had poured into the little boat and it was again threatened with capsizing. The men grabbed the nearest container and baled for their lives. It took an hour of frantic work and once again, *Caird* had a narrow escape.

In the commotion no one noticed that sea had broken into the precious barrel of drinking water. It was badly fouled by the salty sea water.

The hungry, tired and soaked crew of the *Caird* now faced perhaps the worst torture of all – thirst.

Apart from making drinks, they could not cook the hoosh without water. It meant gnawing on raw, dry rations.

Tom tried to filter the brackish water through cloth, but it still tasted horribly salty and made them feel even more thirsty. As days passed, their thirst grew worse. Their lips cracked and tongues were swollen. The situation was desperate.

In spite of this, the *James Caird* was defying the odds and making good progress towards South Georgia. Winds, although very strong, were mostly in their favour and pushing the craft on the correct course to the island.

After two weeks, Skipper calculated they must be near their goal. But the island was nowhere to be seen.

Hopes soared when someone caught sight of a small bird flying overhead. Birds indicated land was nearby. But heavy black clouds and swirling winds which whipped up the sea spray made it impossible to see far ahead.

Suddenly one of the men screamed out, 'Land!'

Strong winds had blown a gaping hole in the clouds and rising out of the sea were the black, snow-topped mountains of South Georgia.

The relief was immense. They had done the impossible, crossing the Southern Ocean in an open boat and defying colossal waves and gales.

But the ocean refused to let them escape without a fight.

Winds blew stronger as the *James Caird* sailed close to the shore. Within a short time a full-scale hurricane was hurled down on the little craft and winds roared to over 130kph (80mph).

The *Caird* was again at the full mercy of the weather. The shore was within reach but landing was impossible because the boat would be smashed onto the rocks in the fierce winds.

The hurricane hammered down on the *Caird* for hours. Only a few miles away in the same waters a large cargo ship sank in the raging storm. All the sailors on board were drowned.

Darkness fell and the storm continued. Some of the *Caird's* planks buckled and split under the strain. Water poured in and the men again baled for their lives throughout a terrible night.

Hopes of better weather were dashed as soon as daylight broke. The storm continued unchecked and even cooking was impossible as 13m (40ft) waves smashed down on the boat.

For ten hours the hurricane hurled itself at the little vessel. Through the odd break in the clouds it was still possible to see glimpses of the mountains and the shore. But landing was still impossible and the weakened men braced themselves for another night at sea.

Luckily the weather improved through the night and daylight revealed a calmer scene. Winds had eased a little and the *Caird* was still afloat. But landing was now vital.

The six men had been at sea for seventeen days, their strength had gone and their thirst was now intolerable. No one would survive another day or night of battering from a Southern Ocean hurricane.

The boat was steered towards the shore but winds were blowing them away from the land. In desperation, the sails were lowered, the men grabbed the oars and started to row inland.

It was grim. All around jagged rocks poked out from the heaving seas. Any clash with the rocks spelt their end.

A narrow passage through the rocks was spotted. At the end of the passage was a beach. It was their chance for survival.

Rowing for their lives, they managed to get close to the gap. They waited for a strong wave. In an instant, the oars were pulled from the water and the next wave carried the boat forward through the opening.

The force of the wave took the *Caird* onto the beach, where it came to a grinding halt on the stones.

It was 522 days – one year and five months – since the men had last set foot on the island of South Georgia.

Chapter 18

MARCH OR DIE

Tom Crean fell out of the *James Caird*, drained and desperately thirsty. He dragged himself to his feet and quickly searched the beach for drinking water.

Only a few feet away Tom spotted a trickle of water running down the rocky slopes from a glacier situated high up the steep cliffs. In seconds the men scrambled to the rock, sank to their knees and began drinking from the ice-cool stream.

After seventeen days in the Southern Ocean the water was like vintage champagne.

The six men were a pitiful sight. Some could barely walk on their shaky legs after being so long at sea. Frostbite, hunger, exhaustion and thirst had taken a heavy toll.

Unloading the *Caird* was the first task but even this light work proved too much. They did not even have the strength to haul the boat out of the water. In haste, the *Caird* was tethered to a rock and Tom cooked a hot meal.

A small cave was found. It was dingy and damp but it offered all the comforts of a five-star hotel to men on the brink of collapse.

They soon slid into their sleeping bags.

It was decided that one man had to stay awake at all times to make sure the *James Caird*, which was still tied to a rock, remained safe through the night. It was a wise move.

Tom was on watch at around 2 o'clock in the morning when a huge wave came crashing onto the shore and pulled the boat away from its mooring. In a flash, Tom leapt into the cold water to catch the rope before the *Caird* drifted out to sea.

Tom's shouts of alarm woke the others from their deep sleep and they rushed to his rescue. Tom was standing up to his neck in the breakers, with freezing waves washing over his head.

Despite the fierce cold and soaking, Tom hung onto the rope as the others plunged into the water to help. Fortunately, the *Caird* was saved, and so too was Tom.

The incident frightened them as they could not afford to lose the boat. They sat, exhausted, through the bitterly cold, wet night hanging onto the boat.

Dawn brought a new crisis. In the scramble to save Tom and prevent the *Caird* drifting out to sea, no one noticed that the craft's rudder had broken off. Without the means of steering, the *Caird* was now reduced to little more than a rowing boat. But rowing was out of the question for the shattered men.

The crisis forced an urgent re-think of their plans. Originally, the intention was to sail the *Caird* to the north side of the island, where the Norwegians kept whaling stations open for most of the year. Help and rescue for the stranded men on Elephant Island waited there.

But the *Caird's* journey had taken the vessel to the south side where there were no inhabitants. Without a rudder the boat could not sail around the island to the whaling stations in the north. Going by sea was now impossible.

The men were in an appalling state. Two of the crew were on the brink of collapse and another was very weak. It was unlikely they would all survive another journey.

The grim facts began to sink in. They could not sail the *Caird* around the island and three of them were too weak to travel.

There was no hope of rescue because no one knew they were there. Staying put meant certain death, both for those in the little cave on South Georgia and for the 22 castaways marooned on Elephant Island.

The only choice was to walk from the south coast to the whaling stations in the north.

It was a daunting prospect. No one before had crossed the interior of South Georgia, which is a mountainous island scattered with massive glaciers and ice-fields.

The rocky mountains of South Georgia are on average over 1.6km (1 mile) high. The highest rises to almost 3.2km (2 miles) and the centre of the island is littered with treacherous glaciers, hazardous crevasses and steep ice slopes.

No one lived in the bleak rocky interior and there was no map to guide the men. Perhaps it was impassable. Only desperate men would attempt such a march into unknown territory.

Only three men were capable of making the trip over the mountains. They were Shackleton, the expedition leader, the navigator, Skipper Worsley and the indestructible Tom Crean. But these men were sailors – not mountaineers.

As the crow flies, the whaling stations were about 48km (30 miles) away. It was decided to move as fast as possible. Only essential items were taken. Everything else was left behind.

Tents and sleeping bags were too heavy to carry. The only equipment they brought was a primus stove, a small cooking pot and fuel for six meals. Each man stuffed a spare sock with enough food for three days.

In addition, they took two compasses, a pair of binoculars, half a box of matches, 15m (50ft) of rope and an adze, which is a carpenter's cutting tool, to act as an ice pick.

Their footwear was a serious problem. Experienced ice travellers like Tom realised that their reindeer fur boots, with flat, smooth soles, would not give a proper grip on the slippery glaciers which they had to cross. An unlucky fall on the glassy surface might mean a broken arm or leg – and probable death.

In an inspired move, screws were tugged from the side of the *James Caird* and hammered through the soles of the boots as makeshift crampons which would provide some grip on the icy slopes. It was the best they could do.

To prepare themselves for the march, the men needed rest and some proper food. Tom turned hunter and found some albatrosses perched in the nearby rocks, which made a fine hot meal for the hungry men.

A better spot was found to camp and the *James Caird* was turned upside down as a shelter against the howling winds. The boat was propped up by rocks and the six sleeping bags were stored underneath. Bits of driftwood were rounded up from the beach to make a large, warming fire. Occasionally, they had a sing-song to cheer themselves up.

Well fed and warm, the men slept soundly and slowly began to recover their much-needed strength.

After a few days, the men made the final preparations. They shook hands with their three comrades staying behind and began their historic march.

It was 3 o'clock in the morning and a splash of moonlight guided their first steps up from the beach and onto the overhanging glacier. A good sign.

Chapter 19

AN HISTORIC TREK

For two hours the men climbed steadily, pausing briefly to inspect what lay ahead.

The track ahead was terrifying. Steep ice slopes led up to a collection of five mountains which barred their way like the knuckles on a clenched fist. One of the peaks had to be crossed to get to whaling stations on the other side.

As dawn drew near a swirling fog blotted out the view ahead and made the travelling even more dangerous. In the gloom, the men walked to the very edge of a wide crevasse without realising the danger. A few more steps would have been fatal.

In the half light it was not possible to see more than a few feet ahead. Quickly the three men decided to link together by rope.

The men walked in single file, with Shackleton leading the procession. From behind Tom Crean and Skipper barked orders about the direction the men should be taking – 'port' for left, 'starboard' for right and 'steady' to continue straight onwards.

Hopes improved as daylight emerged and the fog lifted. In the distance, the men saw a large stretch of water. It looked like a frozen lake, which would be easier to cross than the crevasses or icy slopes.

Anxious to move as quickly as possible, the trio descended onto the lake. But they had been fooled.

The 'lake', which stretched as far as the eye could see, was a bay. The men were gazing out into the open sea, the wrong direction for the whaling stations.

Unhappily the men turned and began to climb back the way they came. Retracing their steps, they climbed back up to the heights to gain a clearer view of the territory ahead. It was precious time lost – time they could not afford.

After six hours of walking, often over soft snow which made the going slow, the men stopped to eat.

This encouraged the men. Shackleton complained that Tom's spoon was bigger than the other two spoons. Quick as a flash, Tom replied, 'Doesn't matter, the Skipper has got a bigger mouth'.

Back on the march, the men approached the knuckle of mountains. The easiest-looking route was chosen and they began to slog uphill. Three hours later they stood at the top of the peak. But the sight ahead was alarming.

The slope below broke away into steep precipices and cliffs which were impossible to cross. Even modern climbers with the latest equipment would have found the descent difficult.

For the second time that morning, the men had to turn round and retrace their steps. More valuable time lost.

At the bottom of the slope Tom cooked again and they prepared to tackle the next climb. This time it was even steeper than the first and they sank deeply in the snow. Climbing was exhausting and they regularly fell to their knees panting for breath.

The sight at the top was even worse than the first peak. Below the land was another muddle of broken ice and fearsome glaciers, riddled with crevasses. Dejected and bitterly disappointed, the men turned around and went back down the icy slope again.

Slowly they managed to reach the third summit where another bitter disappointment stared them in the face. Getting down was impossible. The only choice was to climb down again. More time gone.

It was around 4 o'clock in the afternoon as they began to move back down the mountain. Night was fast approaching when temperatures started to drop sharply. They were at a height of around 1,400m (4,500ft) and fog was creeping over the mountain top.

The men were in real danger of freezing to death. It was vital they get down from the heights as fast as possible.

But the descent was not easy, particularly in the soft, sticky snow which had made the climb up so slow. A desperate situation called for desperate measures.

The answer was to risk sliding down the ice slope like tobogganists.

The 16m (50ft) length of rope was quickly coiled into three circular 'mats'. Shackleton sat at the front and Skipper wrapped his legs around Shackleton's waist. Tom joined behind and wrapped himself round Skipper. They were locked together as one.

In an instant, the three men kicked off and the 'toboggan' hurtled downhill. They gathered speed and the wind whistled past their ears as they plummeted downwards.

Tom, at the back, was hit by the adze and narrowly avoided a bad gash. But they clung together, yelling at the top of their voices as they raced along. No one dared think what would happen if they smashed into a rock.

Luckily the soft snow at the bottom of the slope acted as a brake on their terrifying drop. The trio came to an abrupt stop as they ran into a bank of snow.

Slowly the three men stood up and inspected the damage. They found a few rips in their trousers but otherwise they were safe and well. The free fall lasted about two minutes and no one was sure how far they had travelled. They simply thanked their luck.

They ate and were quickly on their way again. Darkness fell and overhead the moon reappeared. They had been on the march without a proper rest for almost 24 hours.

Fatigue gripped the men. But sleep was impossible – it could mean death in these freezing conditions.

Taking a break at one point, Tom and the Skipper dozed off. Shackleton shook them awake after just five minutes. To make them feel better he told them they had slept for half an hour.

Through the night the three walked slowly but surely and hoped that daylight would bring a sight of the whaling stations. No one was quite sure of their direction, particularly in the dark. But they had to press on.

In the twilight before dawn the men came to the top of a hill and looked down on a bay. It might have been Stromness Bay. If it was, there was a whaling station there.

Tom brewed some hoosh and entertained them with a song. The journey, they thought, was at an end.

But as they plodded on towards the bay, the awful sight of a mighty glacier laced with dangerous crevasses loomed. There was no glacier at Stromness. Their direction was wrong, which meant turning round and going back.

Slowly they climbed another icy slope. At the top they could pick out the mountains, which from memory they knew bordered the whaling stations.

It was about 6.30 in the morning as daylight appeared. Someone thought they heard noise. They thought it was the sound of men getting ready for work at the whaling station. If they were right, the next sound would be heard at precisely 7 o'clock when the factory whistle called the men to work. If they heard the whistle, their journey was over.

Tom, Skipper and Shackleton stood in silence and watched the hands of their watch move slowly towards 7 o'clock.

Tension mounted. Bang on time at 7 o'clock, the silence of the cold morning air was broken by the hooting of a factory whistle in the distance.

It was the first sound they heard from the outside world since leaving South Georgia almost eighteen months earlier. They yelled aloud in triumph.

But there was no time for celebration. All three were in an advanced state of exhaustion, bitterly cold and still miles away from the whaling stations.

Even close to safety, danger was ever present. Once Tom broke through weak ice and plunged into freezing water. He sank up to his waist before being pulled out by the others.

A little later the men came to the top of a ridge. About 750m (2,500ft) below was the busy whaling station at Stromness. They could see ships in the harbour and the tiny specks of men hurrying about their work.

Without thinking the three men began yelling and waving, desperate to attract attention. But their voices were lost in the wind.

Nor did it occur to them that no one would be looking in their direction – no one before had approached Stromness from the interior. Only the desperate would cross South Georgia's inland mountains and glaciers.

The men began to climb down towards Stromness. The slope was very steep and before long they came across a fast-running stream which they followed downwards in the hope of reaching the harbour more quickly.

But to their dismay, the stream came to an abrupt halt at a cliff edge and the freezing water tumbled into a cascading waterfall. The waterfall was about 10m (30ft) long and for a brief moment their spirits fell. Turning and retracing their steps was a terrible prospect when so close to safety.

The time was nearing 3 o'clock in the afternoon and nightfall was coming. Another night in the open was not possible.

The only option was to climb down through the icy cold waterfall.

Tom, the largest of the three men, went first.

A rope was tied to a rock and Tom climbed down slowly. The freezing water drenched him. At one point Tom disappeared under the stream of falling water.

Soaked but happy, the three men were now less than a mile from the whalers.

The men were a strange trio of scarecrows. They had not washed or shaved for months and their hair hung down to their shoulders. Beards were matted with blubber and sea salt.

Frostbite had gnawed at their hands and faces and they gave off a disgusting smell. Their clothes, which they had not changed for months, were in tatters. There was a large hole in the backside of Skipper's trousers and he found an old rusty safety pin to hold them together. His concern was that women might see his ragged pants.

The remarkable march across South Georgia took 36 hours, a day and a half without proper rest or equipment.

Many years later a British army team made the same trip. The troops were fit, well-fed and had modern clothes and equipment. It took them fourteen days to cover the same distance.

The bedraggled, weary men shuffled slowly into the whaling station.

They were unsure how they would be greeted.

Turning a corner near the factory buildings, they bumped into two little boys playing in the street. The boys were horrified and fled in panic.

Minutes later they saw an elderly man. He, too, turned and ran away.

Luckily they soon came across some workers and sailors from the whaling station. The whalers were astonished at the shabby wrecks of human beings standing before them.

The kindly whalers quickly gave the men a hot drink and listened in silence as they heard their unbelievable tale of survival against all the odds.

They told how *Endurance* was crushed by the ice, how 28 men survived for months on an ice-floe, how they crossed the vicious Southern Ocean in an open boat and finally how they walked across the unexplored mountains of South Georgia.

One by one, the tough sailors stepped forward to shake the hands of the three men. One of them commented, 'These are men'.

Chapter 20

RESCUE MISSION

Tom, Skipper and Shackleton, were treated like kings. The whalers found space for them in their own homes and the men had their first hot bath for eighteen months. A clean set of clothes was found for each man, followed by a huge meal and a warm comfortable bed.

Next day a ship went around the island to recover the three men left behind with the *James Caird*. Plans were also made for a much bigger rescue – to get the 22 castaways off the beach at Elephant Island. It was no easy task.

Tom, Skipper and Shackleton spent months trying to reach their stranded comrades camped under the boats on Elephant Island. It was a heartbreaking time.

Three times ships sailed close to the island, but the ice pack prevented them getting close enough to land.

On Elephant Island, the 22 men on the rocky beach feared the worst. Many felt the *James Caird* had sunk while crossing the Southern Ocean and that Tom, Skipper and Shackleton had drowned. Days passed into weeks and weeks into months. Some gave up all hope of rescue.

They battled to survive, killing penguins or seals or scraping limpets off the rocks to eat. Mostly the men sheltered beneath the upturned boats from the rampant 160kph (100mph) winds and fierce blizzards which lashed down upon them.

One of the men, the stowaway, suffered badly from frostbite in the freezing conditions. His boots were not waterproof and the frostbite became so critical that doctors were forced to cut off some of his toes. The operation was performed by flickering candlelight under the boats.

Initially it was hoped Tom, Skipper and Shackleton would return to Elephant Island within three or four weeks. After over four months of isolation all hope seemed gone.

One day, two of the castaways were sitting by the sea's edge searching for shellfish to make the evening meal. One of them looked up and suddenly yelled out, 'Ship O!'

Mayhem broke out. A fire was lit to signal the ship as it came near the beach. The men hugged each other with joy and waved frantically.

A rowing boat was lowered from the ship and it began to move slowly towards the shore. Standing up at the front, clearly visible, were the familiar faces of Tom and Shackleton. All 22 castaways had been saved.

The 28 men from *Endurance* were reunited and taken to Chile in South America, where they received a noisy welcome from thousands of well-wishers. Cheering crowds lined the docks, flags waved and bands played. Parties lasted for days and huge crowds turned up to greet them wherever they went.

But it was time to go home.

The *Endurance* expedition, which had begun so hopefully and almost ended in tragedy, lasted about two years.

In the time the explorers were away the First World War had erupted and millions were dying on the battlefields of Europe. The men from *Endurance*, who had been cut off from civilisation for almost two years, were surely the only people on earth who knew nothing about the war.

War also called on Tom.

Chapter 21

TOM THE POLE

Tom Crean sailed back to Europe and rejoined the navy to fight in the war. Luckily, he survived.

He finally retired from the navy four years later in 1920. His distinguished career lasted 27 years. During that time he rose from the lowest rank of Boy Second Class to Warrant Officer and became one of the greatest Polar explorers of all time.

Tom left the navy and went back home to Ireland. He returned to his village of Anascaul, married a local woman called Nell, raised three daughters and opened a pub. The great traveller, who had spent much of life at the ends of the earth, rarely left his village home again.

Tom never forgot his life in the Antarctic. He called his pub the South Pole Inn in memory of his exploits in the ice and snow. The pub is still open today and people come from all over the world to see the home of Tom, the great explorer and hero of the ice.

But he turned down the chance to go back on another Antarctic expedition. Shackleton wanted to mount another expedition and wanted the reliable and tough Tom to travel with him on the new journey.

It was a difficult decision. Tom loved the ice. But he was 43 years old and decided to put his wife and children first. He told Shackleton, 'I have a long-haired pal now', a reference to his wife, Nell.

He was popular in the village. Locals nicknamed him 'Tom the Pole' and Nell was known as 'Nell the Pole'.

But Tom would never talk about his Polar adventures. He was a modest man who never sought fame or publicity. People came from far away to visit the South Pole Inn to talk about the amazing exploits of Tom Crean. But he remained silent, saying nothing.

The war of independence with the British was being fought as Tom came home from the navy in 1920. Anyone linked with the British was unpopular and Tom had served in the British navy for 27 years, mostly on the three expeditions to the Antarctic.

Tom was a proud Irishman who flew the Irish flag on his sledge when exploring in the Antarctic. But in this difficult period, he felt it was wiser to stay in the background and say nothing about his adventures.

In modern days, Tom would have been a famous celebrity appearing on television and radio, and featuring in newspapers and magazines. But Tom did not want publicity. He never allowed himself to be interviewed.

As a result, few people knew of Tom's incredible life.

The only physical sign of Tom's escapades came when he took off his shoes and socks to cool his feet in the Owenascaul river which runs near his old home. His feet, which had been affected by severe frostbite, were black.

Tom lived the rest of his days quietly in Anascaul, raising his family, walking his dog and puffing gently on his pipe, sitting on the wall outside the South Pole Inn.

In 1938, a few days after his sixty-first birthday, he complained of bad stomach pains and was rushed to hospital in the nearby town of Tralee. It was severe appendix trouble which needed an urgent operation.

But there was no surgeon at Tralee and Tom was driven across country by ambulance to a larger hospital in Cork city. The delay was fatal. His appendix burst and blood poisoning set in.

The indestructible man, who for years had defied the most hostile place on earth, was now at the mercy of a very common ailment. Today it would be a routine operation and there would be little to worry about.

However, Tom fell into a coma, hovering between life and death. And on 27 July 1938 Tom died.

Crowds thronged the village for his funeral. Tom's coffin was proudly carried to his final resting place on the shoulders of friends from Kerry and old navy comrades. He was taken to a tomb in a small cemetery at Ballynacourty in the hills overlooking Anascaul.

A few feet away from the tomb, the Owenascaul River flows gently down the hill and past the South Pole Inn, the home of the great explorer and Antarctic legend, Tom Crean.

TOM CREAN – TIMELINE

1877 20 July   Born near Anascaul, County Kerry, Ireland,
                           the son of Patrick and Catherine Crean

1893 10 July   Runs away from home and enlists in Royal Navy

1901 10 December   Joins Captain Scott's Antarctic exploration ship, *Discovery*

1902 February   Makes first sledging expedition in the Antarctic

1904 February   *Discovery* leaves Antarctic

1910 April   Joins Captain Scott's *Terra Nova* expedition
                           to discover the South Pole

1911 January   *Terra Nova* reaches the Antarctic
         1 November   March to the South Pole starts

1912 4 January   Only 150 miles from South Pole; among last to see
                           Captain Scott alive; starts 750 mile return to base camp
         18 February   Volunteers to walk 35 miles to base camp to save Lt Evans
         19 February   Reaches base hut after 18 hour march
         29 October   Starts search for bodies of Captain Scott's party
         12 November   Discovers Captain Scott's tent and buries bodies

1913 January   *Terra Nova* leaves Antarctica
         26 July   Receives Albert Medal at Buckingham Palace
                           from King George for saving the life of Lt Evans

1914 25 May   Joins Sir Ernest Shackleton's *Endurance* expedition
         1 August   *Endurance* sails from London

1915	19 January	*Endurance* trapped in the Weddell Sea
	27 October	*Endurance* abandoned
	21 November	*Endurance* sinks
1916	9 April	Takes charge of *Stancomb Wills* lifeboat on sea journey to Elephant Island
	15 April	Lands at Elephant Island
	24 April	Sails in *James Caird* to South Georgia
	10 May	Lands at South Georgia
	19 May	Starts overland march across South Georgia
	20 May	Reaches whaling station at Stromness
	30 August	Returns to Elephant Island and rescues 22 castaways
	8 October	Sails for Europe
1917	5 September	Marries Eileen (Nell) Herlihy, Anascaul, Co. Kerry
1918	December	Daughter, Mary born
1920	24 March	Retires from Royal Navy after 27 years service
	December	Daughter Katherine, born
1922	April	Daughter, Eileen born
1924	December	Katherine dies, aged 4
1927		Opens pub, The South Pole Inn, Anascaul, Co. Kerry
1938	27 July	Dies at Bon Secours Hospital, Cork, aged 61

USEFUL INFORMATION

Temperatures

To convert Fahrenheit ° to Celsius °

　　Subtract 32, divide by 1.8 (e.g. 68°F minus 32 divided by 1.8 = 20°C)

Celsius° to Fahrenheit°

　　Multiply by 1.8, add 32 (e.g. 20°C x 1.8 = 36 + 32 = 68°F)

Temperature comparisons

°F	°C
98.4° (body temp)	36.9°
32 (water freezes)	0°
14	-10°
-4	-20°
-22	-30°
-40°	-40°

Distances

To convert

Metres (m) to feet (ft)	multiply by 3.28
Feet (ft) to metres (m)	multiply by 0.30
Metres (m) to yards (yds)	multiply by 1.09
Yards (yds) to metres (m)	multiply by 0.91
Kilometres (km) to miles	multiply by 0.61
Miles to kilometres (km)	multiply by 1.61

Weights

To convert

Pounds (lbs) to kilograms (kgs)	multiply by 0.45
Kilograms (kgs) to pounds (lbs)	multiply by 2.21

FURTHER READING

Books

Alexander, Caroline	*Endurance*, Bloomsbury Publishing,
Fothergill, Alastair	*Life in the Freezer*, BBC Books
Hooper, Meredith	*A is for Antarctica*, Pan Books
Lansing, Alfred	*Endurance*, Weidenfeld
Lonely Planet Guide	*Antarctica*, Lonely Planet,
Mountfield, David	*A History of Polar Exploration*, Hamlyn
Scott, Robert F.	*Scott's Last Journey* (Ed. Peter King), Duckworth
Smith, Michael	*An Unsung Hero – Tom Crean Antarctic Survivor*, The Collins Press

Videos

Tom Crean – Kerryman

In The Ice, Crossing the Line Films, Co. Wicklow, Ireland

90 Degrees South, Herbert Ponting, National Film and Television Archive, 1933: Connoisseur Videos, London, UK

Shackleton: Escape From Antarctica, Crossing The Line Films, Co. Wicklow, Ireland

South, Frank Hurley, National Film and Television Archive, 1919: BFI Video Publishing, London, UK

Websites

Antarctic Circle	www.Antarctic--circle.org
Antarctic Project	www.Asoc.org
British Antarctic Survey	www.Nerc-bas.ac.uk
Heritage Antarctic	www.Heritage-antarctica.org
Scott Polar Research Institute	www.Spri.cam.ac.uk

INDEX